SPACE SCIENCE

PLUTO &
THE DWARF PLANETS

BY NATHAN SOMMER

BELLWETHER MEDIA • MINNEAPOLIS, MN

TM

Are you ready to take it to the extreme? Torque books thrust you into the action-packed world of sports, vehicles, mystery, and adventure. These books may include dirt, smoke, fire, and chilling tales. **WARNING**: read at your own risk.

Library of Congress Cataloging-in-Publication Data

Names: Sommer, Nathan, author.
Title: Pluto & the Dwarf Planets / by Nathan Sommer.
Other titles: Pluto and the Dwarf Planets
Description: Minneapolis, MN : Bellwether Media, Inc., [2019] | Series:
    Torque. Space Science | Audience: Ages 7-12. | Audience: Grades 3 to 7. |
    Includes bibliographical references and index.
Identifiers: LCCN 2018039174 (print) | LCCN 2018040547 (ebook) | ISBN
    9781681036953 (ebook) | ISBN 9781626179776 (hardcover : alk. paper)
Subjects: LCSH: Dwarf planets–Juvenile literature. | Pluto (Dwarf
    planet)–Juvenile literature. | Kuiper Belt–Juvenile literature.
Classification: LCC QB698 (ebook) | LCC QB698 .S66 2019 (print) | DDC
    523.49/22–dc23
LC record available at https://lccn.loc.gov/2018039174

Editor: Rebecca Sabelko   Designer: Andrea Schneider

Printed in the United States of America, North Mankato, MN.

TABLE OF CONTENTS

A CHANGING PLANET

It is August 24, 2006. Astronomers vote to change the meaning of a planet. They decide planets must orbit a star and be round. They must be able to push objects out of their orbits.

The astronomers decide Pluto is no longer a true planet. It becomes one of five smaller dwarf planets. The solar system will never be the same again!

PLUTO

WHAT ARE DWARF PLANETS?

   Dwarf planets are too small to be planets. But they are too large to be satellites. They are round and orbit stars. But they do not have enough gravity to be considered true planets. They cannot push or pull space matter in or out of their orbits.

CERES

HAUMEA

ERIS

MAKEMAKE

PLUTO

FUN FACT

GOBLIN PLANET

Scientists announced a new dwarf planet in
October 2018. It is on the very edge of the
solar system. Its nickname is The Goblin!

There are five known dwarf planets
in the solar system. But astronomers think
there could be many more! Eris and Pluto
are the largest. Both are more than
1,400 miles (2,253 kilometers) across.

Pluto is the most well known. It spins
on its side in the opposite direction of
most planets.

DWARF PLANETS VS. EARTH SIZE

PLUTO ERIS CERES MAKEMAKE

EARTH HAUMEA

A TOWERING PEAK

Ceres's mountain Ahuna Mons is similar to the height of mountains on Earth. Ahuna Mons reaches 3 miles (4.8 kilometers) into the sky!

Ahuna Mons

Ceres is the smallest. It is around 590 miles (950 kilometers) across. Its tiny size also makes it an asteroid.

Haumea and Makemake are about the same size as each other. Haumea is shaped like a football because it spins very fast. Makemake is the second-brightest object in the entire solar system!

CERES

HOW DID THE DWARF PLANETS FORM?

The solar system formed 4.6 billion years ago. Gravity pulled dust and gas together to form the planets. Leftover debris was blasted into space. This created the Kuiper Belt.

Some of the debris in the Kuiper Belt came together and formed rocky cores. Gravity pulled in gases and other debris around each core to form the dwarf planets.

NOT THE ONLY ONE

Astronomers have found nine solar systems similar to the Kuiper Belt across the universe. That opens the door to many more possible dwarf planets!

ILLUSTRATION OF OBJECTS IN THE KUIPER BELT

CHARON

Pluto gained five moons. Its largest
moon is Charon. Charon orbits Pluto at
the same speed that Pluto spins. Charon
always hovers over the same spot on Pluto.

MAKEMAKE AND ITS MOON

Two moons orbit Haumea. Makemake and Eris each have one very small moon. Makemake's moon is thought to be as small as 100 miles (161 kilometers) across!

WHERE ARE THE DWARF PLANETS?

Most dwarf planets are found in the Kuiper Belt. This area is around 3 billion miles (4.8 billion kilometers) from Earth. But Ceres is found in the asteroid belt between Mars and Jupiter.

All the dwarf planets except Ceres orbit the Sun slowly because they are so far away. Pluto takes 248 years to orbit the Sun. Eris takes 557 years!

LOCATION OF THE DWARF PLANETS

ERIS

HAUMEA

PLUTO

KUIPER BELT

MAKEMAKE

ASTEROID BELT

CERES

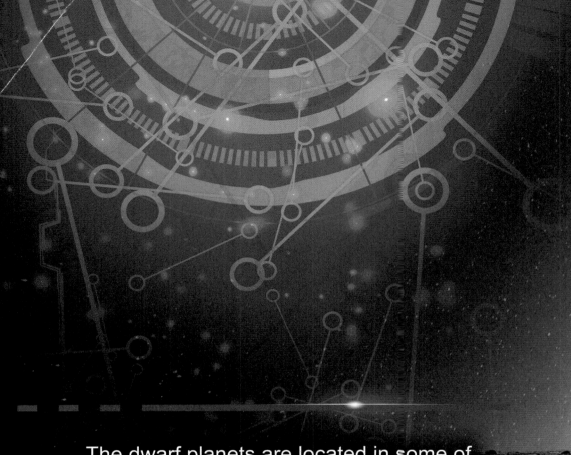

The dwarf planets are located in some of the solar system's coldest areas. Pluto often hits temperatures of around -375 degrees Fahrenheit (-226 degrees Celsius). Its surface has mountains and valleys of water ice.

Pluto's orbit crosses paths with the similarly icy Eris. Sometimes, Eris's thin atmosphere will condense as frost on its surface.

ILLUSTRATION OF PLUTO
AS SEEN FROM CHARON

MOUNTAINS AND
ICE ON PLUTO

WHY DO WE STUDY THE DWARF PLANETS?

Dwarf planets are missing some important elements to become true planets. Astronomers want to know more about why they are different from true planets. They also want to discover how many exist.

The NASA spacecraft, *New Horizons*, will complete flybys of the dwarf planets into the 2020s. There may be hundreds more to be discovered!

LONELY DWARF PLANETS

Only Pluto and Ceres have been visited by spacecraft so far. *New Horizons* studied Pluto and Charon. *Dawn* has been orbiting Ceres since 2015.

NEW HORIZONS SPACECRAFT

GLOSSARY

asteroid—a small, rocky object that orbits the Sun

asteroid belt—a part of space between Mars and Jupiter where many asteroids orbit the Sun

astronomers—people who study space

atmosphere—the gases that surround planets and dwarf planets

condense—to change from a gas to a liquid

cores—the innermost parts of planets

debris—leftover materials

flybys—spacecraft flights that do not land but are close enough to collect scientific information

gravity—the force that pulls objects toward one another

Kuiper Belt—a disc-shaped area surrounding the solar system that is home to many comets, asteroids, and other small, icy space matter

matter—the material something is made of

NASA—National Aeronautics and Space Administration; NASA is a U.S. government agency responsible for space travel and exploration.

orbit—to move around something in a fixed path

satellites—objects that orbit planets and asteroids

TO LEARN MORE

AT THE LIBRARY

Lawrence, Riley. *Exploring Pluto and Other Dwarf Planets*. New York, N.Y.: KidHaven Publishing, 2018.

Rathburn, Betsy. *Planets*. Minneapolis, Minn.: Bellwether Media, 2018.

Scott, Elaine. *To Pluto and Beyond: The Amazing Voyage of New Horizons*. New York, N.Y.: Viking, 2018.

ON THE WEB

FACTSURFER

Factsurfer.com gives you a safe, fun way to find more information.

1. Go to www.factsurfer.com.

2. Enter "Pluto and the dwarf planets" into the search box.

3. Click the "Surf" button and select your book cover to see a list of related web sites.

INDEX